The Little
Book of
Kindness

To my Mum and Dad,
who have always led by example.

The Little
Book of
Kindness

Connect with others,
be happier, transform your life

Dr David Hamilton

An Hachette UK Company
www.hachette.co.uk

First published in Great Britain in 2019 by Gaia Books,
an imprint of Octopus Publishing Group Ltd
Carmelite House
50 Victoria Embankment
London EC4Y 0DZ
www.octopusbooks.co.uk

Distributed in the US by Hachette Book Group,
1290 Avenue of the Americas, 4th and 5th Floors, New York, NY 10104

Distributed in Canada by Canadian Manda Group
664 Annette Street, Toronto, Ontario, Canada M6S 2C8

ISBN 978-1-85675-391-3

A CIP catalogue record for this book is available from the British Library.

Printed and bound in China.

10 8 6 4 2 1 3 5 7 9

Commissioning Editor: Leanne Bryan
Art Director: Juliette Norsworthy
Senior Editor: Alex Stetter
Designer and Illustrator: Abi Read
Copy Editor: Helen Ridge
Production Controller: Emily Noto

Contents

Introduction:
What is Kindness?

"Kindness is an honest,
heartfelt expression."

Kindness requires little explanation. We all know what being kind is, whether it's because we tend to be kind ourselves, or because we've received kindness, or even because we know what it's like not to receive kindness.

In a nutshell, kindness is an honest, heartfelt expression. It can be a thought, a word or an act that is motivated by a desire to help.

It sometimes takes effort. It can "cost" us energy, time, sometimes money. But regardless of the cost, we try to be kind because it's the right thing to do.

Experience teaches us that being kind is important, from the smiles (or sometimes relief) on people's faces when we help them to the utterances of gratitude. We know that kindness matters to the people we help. And we know from being the receivers of kindness how much difference a helping hand can make. Who hasn't come to know the relief when someone takes a difficult situation off their hands, or when someone steps in to save the day, or even when someone is nice when others are not?

The Fabric of Life

Kindness is like glue. It's a glue that holds people together. It even holds society together. In my opinion, were it not for kindness, the fabric of society would unravel. It's the multitude of small gestures, acts of assistance, support, guidance, a listening ear, even a cup of tea, that help us get through our days intact and that hold the wider fabric together.

At the very least, without kindness, society would be more hardened. Kindness softens things. It makes them simpler and clearer. And by soft, I don't mean weak. It can take strength to be kind when others are not. Kindness can call for courage. It can be through patience or forgiveness, or even standing up for someone (or for an animal) or standing up for what is right. Kindness sometimes moves us out of our comfort zone, but we move anyway because we know that what we are saying or doing is right.

It can take courage to buck the trend, to help another instead of one's self, to do what feels right rather than what is expected, or to be kind instead of trying to prove a point. But regardless of whether a kind act softens things or rests on strength and courage, it is all of the stitches that make a fabric strong. We're all part of the fabric of life.

Start with Empathy

In an increasingly busy world, let us pause to consider the needs of those around us and in the wider community or world. For even though it is in our nature to be kind, it is easily forgotten amid the demands many of us face in the modern world. Kindness often starts with empathy, to feel or share another's pain. Empathy moves us into kindness.

Our world is becoming more interconnected and seemingly smaller. The currency of the future is not euros, dollars or yuan. It is empathy – the ability to understand and relate to another, to understand the needs of others, to understand what life is like for them, to share their pain. Through empathy, real communication becomes possible. Only through empathy can we actually solve our problems – together.

Empathy is the path to knowing what type of kindness to show.

In the pages that follow, I aim to offer a unique perspective on the discussion of kindness. I wish to show that kindness is more than something we do. It has physical effects!

I wish to tell you what these are and why they occur, and, in so doing, I hope that you will share the knowledge with others, because the more we talk about kindness in one way or another, the more we *do* kindness. And the more we do kindness, the more everyone benefits.

1. The Biology of Kindness

Kindness is more than something that we do. Kindness has physical effects on the brain, the heart, the immune system and throughout the body in many different ways.

Kindness is the Opposite of Stress

Most people are familiar with stress. If I were to ask you, "What is the opposite of stress?" you would probably say that it is peace, calm, feeling chilled out or some other variation. Those answers make sense at first, but they are not the opposite of stress. They are the *absence* of stress. The opposite of stress, in terms of many of its physical effects, is kindness.

It's all to do with feelings. It's because of how being kind makes you feel.

It's the feelings of stress that produce stress hormones such as adrenalin and cortisol. They don't just appear in our bodies when there's a potentially stressful event looming.

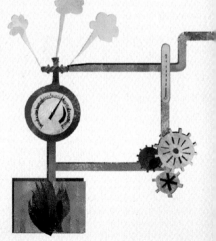

"Just as stress produces stress hormones, kindness produces kindness hormones."

Our feelings about the event produce the stress hormones. The same set of circumstances might be pleasing for one person, for example, but stressful for another. Most events are generally neutral. Our feelings about them are not.

When you are being kind or someone is kind to you, it feels very different from stress. The warm and connected feelings that accompany being kind produce a different kind of hormone. They produce the "kindness hormone", otherwise known as oxytocin.

The kindness hormone, oxytocin, goes by a few other names too:

-  Cuddle chemical
- Hugging hormone
- Hug drug (hugs produce it)
- Molecule of kindness
- Love hormone (it is made abundantly when we feel love)

Not only are the feelings associated with kindness opposite to the feelings associated with stress, they also produce opposite effects in the body.

What Stress Does

Increases blood pressure

Damages the cardiovascular system

Can make people unhappy

Suppresses the immune system

Tenses the nervous system

Increases inflammation

Can trigger depression

What Kindness Does

Reduces blood pressure

Protects the cardiovascular system (kindness is "cardioprotective")

Makes people happy

Boosts the immune system

Relaxes the nervous system

Reduces inflammation

Can be an antidote to depression

An Antidote to Stress

In a study at Yale School of Medicine, researcher Emily Ansell enlisted 77 volunteers to complete a daily assessment for two weeks.[1] She asked them to record any stressful events that happened to them that day, for example at work and at home, regarding their health and relationships. The total number was taken as a numerical measure of their level of stress. They were also asked to record their kind acts, such as holding open a door or offering assistance to someone who needed help. The total number was taken as a measure of a person's kind behaviour. They also rated their mental health each day, which gave a measure of positive and negative emotions.

When she examined the data, Ansell found that on days when the volunteers had done:

- More acts of kindness, their stress levels came down and they experienced less negative emotion

- Fewer acts of kindness, their stress levels went up and their negative emotion was higher too

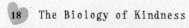

As kindness went up, stress went down — a bit like a seesaw.

It wasn't that being kind meant that stressful things didn't occur — we all know that life happens. Instead, being kind somehow buffered the effects of stressful events. In effect, being kind took some of the "sting" out of them. Kindness seemed to be an antidote to stress.

Kindness Changes the Brain

Kindness is more than something you do that makes you feel nice, it also impacts the brain...physically.

The brain is often described by neuroscientists as being like a muscle. Just as a muscle grows when we exercise it, so do brain regions when we exercise them. The phenomenon of brain growth is known as "neuroplasticity".

Feeling love, kindness and compassion consistently is the brain's equivalent of exercising a muscle consistently. Just as our biceps or glutes grow if we work out, so specific regions of the brain grow if we work them out with love, kindness and compassion. These regions are the insula (empathy region) and the left side of the prefrontal cortex (compassion region and seat of positive emotion).

If we take these "muscles" to the gym – that is, if we are kind or show love, empathy or compassion – they grow like muscles do. If we stop exercising them, they shrink, just like muscles shrink if you don't use them. "Use it or lose it" is the phrase scientists use.

Stress produces physical changes in the brain too, but because stress works out stress regions of the brain, they grow instead.

But if we practise kindness instead of stress, the stress regions of the brain shrink, just like a muscle shrinks when we stop using it as much.

The brain is not as hardwired as people assume. It changes according to how you consistently move, behave, think and feel.

Practising kindness makes the "kindness muscles" in the brain grow bigger and stronger.

EXERCISE:

The Loving-kindness Meditation

This Tibetan Buddhist practice also goes by the name of *metta bhavana*. In the Pali language, *metta* means "love" (in the universal, non-romantic sense), kindness and friendliness. While practising this meditation, we are encouraged to generate feelings of love, kindness and compassion for all beings. Research indicates that the practice produces physical changes in the brain. In particular, it causes the empathy and compassion regions of the brain to grow.[2]

1 Start by saying the following three times (usually in your head): "May I be filled with loving kindness, and be well, peaceful and at ease, happy and free of suffering."

2 Then swap "I" for the name of someone you're close to, such as a partner, child, friend or other loved one, and say the line three times.

3 Next, swap this name for a "neutral person", that is, someone you're neither close to nor distant from,

perhaps a neighbour you don't know well, or a work colleague with whom you have little interaction, or the person who delivers your post. Say the line three times.

4 Then, swap this person for a "difficult person". This might be someone you have a negative emotional charge toward, someone who causes you stress, from the present or past. It might be someone you don't like or you regard as selfish. It could even be a politician that you have a problem with. Say the line three times.

5 Lastly, swap this person for "all sentient beings", which includes people, animals, birds, fish, insects, again saying the line three times.

This series of "*I, loved one, neutral person, difficult person, all sentient beings*" corresponds to one cycle. You can do as many cycles as you wish, starting each one with yourself: "May I be filled with loving kindness…" For subsequent cycles, you can change the loved one, neutral person or difficult person each time or keep them the same.

Wired to be Kind

Look around you – kindness is everywhere. Yet it's quite common for people to think that humans are inherently selfish, and some even refer to our "selfish genes".

But we don't have a genetic disposition to be selfish. The term "selfish genes" merely refers to the process

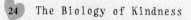

The Biology of Kindness

of genetic replication, where the "selfish" goal of the DNA molecule is to reproduce. In actual fact, over millions of years, this process has resulted in a species whose natural tendency is to be kind. We are genetically *wired* to be kind.

This has happened through natural selection. Over millions of years, the ancestral children of parents with "kind" genes were more likely to survive due to being better cared for than children of non-caring parents who did not have those genes. These surviving children were thus born with kind genes themselves, which they inherited from their caring parents and then subsequently passed onto their own children, who were also genetically inclined to care for their children, and so on. Nature "selects" kind genes because they are most conducive to survival.

Similarly, our ancient ancestors who helped each other, shared their food and built communities based on cooperation were more likely to survive and pass on their "helpful genes" than those who were inclined to look out for themselves. Thus, these communities produced offspring who also had the natural tendency to help each other and share their food.

The Kindness Gene

In studying the kindness hormone, oxytocin, scientists found that it comes in a number of slightly different forms, like many shades of one colour.[3] They discovered that it accounted for slight natural variations in people's kind behaviour and motivations. Some people have a specific shade of the gene, for example, that makes them a little more likely to be kind in a given set of circumstances than another person with a different shade of the gene.

That these variations exist and are related to a person's tendency for kindness offers enough proof that the oxytocin gene is the kindness gene.

And the important thing is that we all have the kindness gene, regardless of its shade. There are no exceptions.

At approximately 500 million years old, the kindness gene is actually one of the oldest in the human genome. Throughout that span of time, it has integrated itself into many key systems of the body, making our growth and health partially dependent upon kindness.

This is why kindness affects our health in so many ways – it impacts the heart, the immune system, mind and emotions, brain chemistry and structure, skin, muscles, the nervous system, even the gut – and why a lack of kindness and connection tends to have negative health consequences.

Kindness and Children

Children need love, affection, responsiveness, play, touch. They also need kindness. When these things are missing, it affects their growth – physically and mentally.

For every three months a child spends in an institution, such as an orphanage, he loses a month of growth. That's a one-third drop in his growth rate because he is not being properly cared for. Bones grow more slowly, the head circumference tends to be smaller, even the internal organs are smaller.

Much of this research emerged from the Bucharest Early Intervention Project (BEIP) in Romania at the beginning of this century, which studied the impact that growing up in an orphanage had on the growth and development of children.[4] The project scientists found that institutionalized children developed at slower rates, both physically and mentally, and even had deficits in brain development.

Being loved and well cared for is critical for children. The study also found that when the children were fostered, they caught up in many of these measures. The critical time for fostering, however, was before the age of two. After that age, it was much more difficult for the children's development to approach normal levels. But if the children were placed in foster care or adopted early enough, their growth and development accelerated.

The bottom line is that children need love, affection, responsiveness, play, touch and kindness. So, too, do adults. It's because we're all wired that way.

Just as kindness is good for our health, the absence of it can be damaging.

2. The Benefits of Kindness

Kindness has side effects, and it turns out that all of them are beneficial.

Kindness Makes Us Happier

The "helper's high" is a term that was coined by Allan Luks in his book *The Healing Power of Doing Good* (1992). He analysed data from populations of people who did volunteer work and found that 95 percent of them reported that helping others made them feel good. We get a natural high from helping.

It's the common experience of most people. Scientists have since investigated the phenomenon in many different ways. For example, scientists at the University of British Columbia gave people money in the morning and asked them to spend it either on themselves or on others throughout the day. They found that those who spent the money on others tended to be happier by the end of the day than those who spent it on themselves.

A study led by psychologist Sonja Lyubomirsky, from the University of California at Riverside, asked volunteers to conduct five acts of kindness per week for six weeks.[5] They chose to do things like give blood, help friends, visit an elderly person, even pay for someone's parking. When she compared the volunteers with a control group (people not doing the acts of kindness), she found that being kind had made the volunteers happier.

Numerous other studies have found the same thing. Being kind makes us happier.

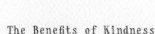

The Kindness Pill - an Antidote to Depression

I suffered from depression back in 1998. I found myself withdrawing from others. I didn't feel comfortable around people at all. I found it difficult to converse and just wanted to be at home by myself, where it felt less stressful. Yet, at home, I often found myself crying and sleeping a lot in an effort to try to pass the time.

When we're depressed, the tendency is to withdraw from people and withdraw into ourselves, yet research suggests doing the opposite can be extremely beneficial; that is, getting out and helping others. It's counterintuitive: why would you want to spend time helping other people when you're the one who needs the help?

When we focus on the needs of another, it takes us out of ourselves. It suspends our focus on how we are feeling. It taps into a deeper part of ourselves. As good feelings of helping others rise to the surface, they displace some of the pain. In this way, good feelings can learn to flow again like magma from a volcano, continually rising up from inside.

Many people have found this formula extremely helpful. In helping others, they have helped – and healed – themselves. In the late 18th and early 19th centuries, moral treatment was a popular way of helping people with mental health problems.[6] As a reaction against the seemingly inhumane and brutal asylums of the time, where depressed people were locked away and treated as "mad", William Tuke, a Quaker, founded the York Retreat, in York in the north of England, where those with mental health issues came to live.

The retreat was run on the principles of kindness, order and trust, with the treatment of patients personalized, benevolent and compassionate. Patients lived like a family and were encouraged to help each other and the "family". The trust, autonomy, respect and kindness that they were shown, and encouraged to show each other as part of the treatment, aided healing and encouraged the building of self-esteem.

The retreat was so successful that the model spread to the US, where it gained popularity and spread through the country, only to decline gradually a hundred or so years later with the advent of pharmaceutical treatments.

There is renewed interest now, though. Scientists have rekindled work in the area and found lots of modern evidence that kindness can be an antidote to depression. For example, a University of Texas study of over 3,500 people found that those who did voluntary work had much lower rates of depression than those who didn't.[7]

Kindness is like a pill, but you don't need medical insurance to afford it. It's a special type of pill, though. It's not one you take yourself. You have to give it away for it to work.

It's free, yet the "profits" are huge and are distributed between the giver and the receiver.

"When we focus on the needs of another, it takes us out of ourselves."

Kindness Produces Happy Chemicals in the Brain

It's been suggested that being kind might boost the brain's natural versions of morphine and heroin, known as endogenous opiates, which is why we get a "helper's high". Kindness is also believed to increase levels of dopamine and serotonin.

Kindness also increases levels of the kindness hormone in the brain. Stress and fear are known to restrict happiness, but the kindness hormone can reduce stress and fear. In a study by scientists at University College London, volunteers were preconditioned through electric shocks to associate stress and fear with certain faces, while having an MRI scan, and the scientists observed any activation in the stress and fear regions of the brain.[8]

Half of the volunteers were then given a dose of oxytocin and the other half a placebo (salt water). Shortly afterward, they all went back into the MRI scanner and were shown the faces again. Those who had received the placebo had a negative reaction to the faces and a high activation in the stress and fear brain regions, yet those who had

received oxytocin had a much reduced activation and even rated the faces as likeable.

Like a kind of dimmer switch, the kindness hormone had actually turned down the stress and fear regions of the brain. As a consequence, kindness makes us feel happier.

Count Kindnesses

Keep a note of all the kind things you do and say over the next month. Use a nice notebook – either a new one that feels good or put an attractive cover on an existing one. Make the exercise special.

You might have to make notes a few times a day, lest you forget what you did. It's OK if you forget some things but

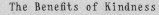

try to jot down most of what you do. You can also make a note of how you feel or any consequences you observe. You could record numerous different kind acts, such as when you:

- Pay someone a compliment

- Hold open a door for someone

- Genuinely wish someone a nice day

- Smile to reassure someone or show them that you are listening

- Make others tea, coffee or something to eat

- Sit with a friend who needs to talk

- Listen to make someone feel validated

- Help others at work, even if that help is expected of you; you can still be doing it because you're aware that it is helping the person

- Give money or food to a homeless person

The purpose of this exercise is not to be intentionally kinder, although that might happen naturally. If so, go with it. The main purpose is simply to observe your normal self and notice how many kindnesses you do. This exercise is based on research that found that counting kindnesses improved people's happiness and self-esteem.

Kindness Keeps the Heart Healthy

The kindness hormone has powerful effects throughout the cardiovascular system. For example, it causes the smooth muscle cells that line our arteries to relax. As a result, blood pressure is reduced and more blood can reach tissues and organs.

The reason these things happen is because the kindness hormone turns up levels of nitric oxide in our arteries, which is one of the most important substances in the human body. Nitric oxide is a blood pressure regulator, and some popular heart drugs are simple systems of delivering it into the arteries. When blood pressure is high, nitric oxide relaxes the walls of the arteries and the arteries dilate (expand), which causes blood pressure to come down. Dr Louis Ignarro, who received a Nobel Prize for his work on nitric oxide, calls it the "miracle molecule".

As a consequence of the fact that kindness produces oxytocin, which then produces nitric oxide, which reduces blood pressure, it means that kindness is "cardioprotective" – it protects the cardiovascular system.[9]

"Kindness is 'cardioprotective' – it protects the cardiovascular system."

This explains why people in a relationship characterized by love and affection tend to have healthier hearts than those in a relationship characterized by hostility or aggression.

A study of 150 married couples conducted by scientists at the University of Utah, for example, found that those with the most hostile relationships had high levels of coronary artery calcification (a hardening of the arteries), while those whose relationships were characterized by more displays of love, kindness, affection and emotional warmth had the healthiest arteries.[10]

How the Kindness Hormone Cleans the Blood

The kindness hormone also helps to maintain clear arteries by keeping at bay two of the processes that can lead to cardiovascular disease: oxidative stress, caused by free radicals, and inflammation.

In one study, scientists at the University of Miami took cells from the arteries and immune system and subjected them to stress in the lab.[11] They noted high levels of oxidative stress and inflammation, as expected. But when they repeated the experiment in the presence of oxytocin, the levels were much lower. In effect, oxytocin was cleaning these substances out of the blood by acting as an antioxidant and an anti-inflammatory.

The Roseto Effect

The blood pressure-lowering effects of the kindness hormone, together with its antioxidant and anti-inflammatory effects, are most likely responsible for what is known as the Roseto Effect.

Roseto is a town on the Eastern Seaboard of the United States. There was a national census in the 1960s and, astonishingly, given the typically high rates of heart disease in the US, it found that not a single person in Roseto under the age of 45 had ever died of a heart attack.

After much investigation, it turned out that the seeming immunity to heart disease was a consequence of:

💜 A strong sense of community

💜 Positive social contact

💜 Sharing

💜 People looking out for and helping each other, that is to say, being kind

It wasn't a real immunity in the sense that people were genetically predisposed to have more resilient hearts, it was simply the protective effects of community, kindness and positive social contact, which generate the kindness hormone, that did the job.

Residents interacted with each other frequently. They stopped to speak on the street. They enjoyed regular community events. The elders knew the middle names of the kids playing in the neighbourhoods. Many households had four generations of family living under the same roof.

As time went on, however, as younger residents grew up and left the town, and people who had grown up in other parts of the country moved in, the way of life in Roseto began to resemble that of the rest of the US. Thus, in 1970, the first ever death by heart attack in a person under 45 was recorded in Roseto. Nowadays, the heart disease stats for Roseto are much the same as for the rest of the US.

But the protective effect that community, positive social contact and kindness can have on the heart is still known to this day as the Roseto Effect. I like to call it the power of "kind-nnection" (kindness and connection).

How to Improve Your "Kind-nnection"

1 Take a piece of paper and draw a line down the centre, or open a journal on a blank double page.

2 On the left-hand side, write about your relationships with others and your sense of connection with them. Give a score for your relationship with each person on a scale of 0–10, where zero represents no connection and 10 is a warm, fulfilling sense of connection. Include your loved ones, friends and even colleagues.

3 On the right-hand side, write about how you can improve these relationship connections. Set realistic goals. For example, if you scored one relationship as a 3, then you might set a goal of taking it up to a 6 or 7. So you would then write about practical steps that you could take to make such an improvement.

The key is the steps that *you* intend to take. This is not about what the other person needs to say or do, but what *you* need to say or do.

A Hug a Day Keeps the Cardiologist Away

Hugging produces the kindness hormone. It's one of the reasons why oxytocin is also sometimes referred to as the "cuddle chemical", "hugging hormone" or the "hug drug".

A study conducted by scientists at the University of North Carolina at Chapel Hill, in which 59 women were asked to count the number of hugs they had experienced over a month, found that those who had experienced the most hugs had the highest levels of the kindness hormone.[12] They also had the lowest blood pressure.

In another study at the same university, 38 couples were asked to report on how much warm emotional contact they had, which included hugs. Again, the scientists found that those who had the most amount of warm contact had the highest oxytocin levels and also the lowest blood pressure.

Given the protective role that oxytocin plays in the cardiovascular system, we might say that a hug a day keeps the cardiologist away.

The Give Hugs Challenge

Set yourself a target of how many hugs you will collect each day for a set time period. It might be a few days, a week or even a month. You might set yourself a target of one, two or three hugs per day, for example, depending on your environment or circumstances, or you might go for a really adventurous number that calls upon you to stretch out of your comfort zone or be extra creative.

Challenge some of your friends or family members to do the challenge too.

You could even add a social media aspect to the challenge: "I challenge [name of person] to collect seven hugs a day for the next three days", for example. You can change the

numbers to suit the person or situation. At the end of the challenge, that person challenges someone else, who then challenges someone else, and so on. It's a bit of fun, but it's healthy fun and good for the heart.

Be Kind to Animals

Being kind to animals has much the same effects on the heart as being kind to humans. Statistically, people who have animals in their family are likely to have lower rates of hypertension than those who don't. They also tend to have lower cholesterol and a more relaxed nervous system.

A study titled "Pet ownership and cardiovascular risk: a scientific statement from the American Heart Association" analysed the data from a large number of published studies and concluded that "pet ownership, particularly dog ownership, is probably associated with decreased cardiovascular disease risk", and that it was likely that pet ownership was responsible for the lower risk.[13]

According to some research, the chances of people who have had a heart attack experiencing a second one within a year is 400 percent less if they own a dog.[14] It is normal to assume that this reduction is due to the exercise that people get by walking their dogs. This is most definitely part of the reason, but not the only part.

It's the quality of the relationship with the animal that matters, just as it is with humans. Married people have lower rates of heart disease than single people, but only when the marriage is a good one. Having a dog is likely to have little effect on the heart unless a person has a good-quality relationship with the dog.

In other words, being kind to an animal, caring for it and playfully interacting with it matter much more than its physical presence at home. It's the relationship that counts.

Indeed, research suggests that a large part of the 400 percent effect is likely to be due to the production of the kindness hormone as we play with our dogs. While monitoring people interacting with their dogs for 30 minutes, scientists at Azabu University in Japan found that the owners' oxytocin levels rose at the rate of around 10 percent per minute over that period.[15] They increased in the dogs too, at around 5 percent per minute.

It just so happens that much of this kind of cardiovascular research has been done with dogs, probably because of the known link between exercise and the reduced risk of cardiovascular disease. The same type of effect is likely to be found as we show kindness toward, and form bonds with, other animals. Earlier research with rabbits showed that when the animals were lovingly stroked on a regular basis, they were significantly more resistant to heart disease than rabbits that were not.

Kindness Boosts the Immune System

The Mother Teresa Effect is the name given to a study that found that watching Mother Teresa being kind and compassionate increased a person's immune function.[16]

In the study at Harvard University, 132 volunteers watched a 50-minute video of Mother Teresa on the streets of Calcutta (Kolkata) carrying out acts of kindness and compassion. They had their immune systems sampled before and after they watched the video.

The scientists measured levels of a substance called secretory immunoglobulin A (S-IgA) in the saliva. This immune system antibody is considered a reliable indicator of overall immune function or efficiency. After watching the video, the volunteers' S-IgA levels increased quite considerably, and stayed elevated for hours afterward as the volunteers reminisced about specific moving elements in the film they had watched.

Watch Inspirational Movies

Watch inspirational movies from time to time. Select those that are moving, that inspire with acts of love, compassion or kindness. For example:

Forrest Gump	*Pay It Forward*
It's a Wonderful Life	*The Truman Show*
Seven Pounds	*The Pursuit of Happyness*
The Blind Side	*Good Will Hunting*
Wonder	*It Could Happen to You*

The feelings generated produce the kindness hormone.

You may get the same effect from watching documentaries that demonstrate kindness.

You can also watch and share videos on social media that show acts of kindness or compassion.

Kindness Slows Aging

Is kindness better than Botox? It may sound a bit out-there to suggest it but, in some quite natural ways, kindness might give Botox a run for its money.

We all know that stress speeds up aging. One of the reasons for this is that mental and emotional stress increases oxidative stress (see page 42) in our cells, that is to say, the damaging effects of free radicals, which can be produced by UV light, diet or stress.

However, the kindness hormone is an antioxidant, which means that it fights oxidative stress. This is another one of the ways that kindness has an opposite effect to stress.

Oxidative stress is one of the aging processes of the skin.

It's much the same process that causes a picked apple to wrinkle when it is left out for a few weeks, although an apple wrinkles much faster than human skin.

Antioxidants are recommended in our diet because they counter oxidative stress, especially in the heart and arteries, where it is linked with heart disease, and in the brain, where it is linked with memory loss and Alzheimer's. It's also the reason why there are antioxidants in some face creams.

Studies on skin cells show that when they are stressed, oxidative stress increases.[17] But when there is plenty of the kindness hormone around, oxidative stress is considerably reduced. As it does in the cardiovascular system, the kindness hormone plays the role of a powerful antioxidant in the skin, thus slowing the rate at which skin cells age.

The important thing is that we cannot eat or drink the kindness hormone. The only way to get it into our skin is to produce it internally, and one of the best ways to do that is by being kind.

So, could kindness challenge Botox? Perhaps! Think of it the other way: we age much faster under stress – usually quite visibly. Being the physiological opposite of stress, kindness slows the process.

"The kindness hormone plays the role of a powerful antioxidant in the skin."

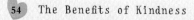

EXERCISE:

An Oxytocin Meditation

The following meditation is designed to generate some of the feelings that are known to produce oxytocin: love, warmth and connection.

1 Think of three people (or animals) whom you love or have fond memories of. They could be from your present or past or even no longer alive.

2 Close your eyes and start to imagine a pink ball of light emanating from the area of your heart. Let this represent the love or gratitude you feel for the first person (or animal).

3 Imagine taking it in your hands and sending it through the air to them. Imagine it reaching them and entering the area of their heart.

4 Now imagine you are with the person (or animal).

5 How do you feel about them? Tell them. Say what you would like to say, as an expression of your love, compassion or gratitude toward them. Say or do what you need to, so that you feel a sense of warmth or

The Benefits of Kindness   55

connection. You may even recall a memory, a time when you felt a warm connection with them, perhaps a fond memory of a time well spent. Relive some of this memory.

6 When you have said what you wanted to say or recalled what you wished to recall, thank the person (or animal) for being in your life.

7 Now bring your attention back to your own heart area. Take a few relaxing breaths and imagine a second ball of pink light emanating from your heart that represents the love or gratitude you feel for the second person (or animal).

8 Visualize as before, then return your attention to your heart and imagine a third ball of pink light, sending it to the third person (or animal) and visualizing as before.

9 Finally, return your attention to the area of your heart. Relax and breathe comfortably for a few minutes and then open your eyes.

The Benefits of Kindness

Kindness Improves Relationships: the Magic Ratio

We tend to like people who are kind to us. That much is obvious to most of us. But research on relationships finds that kindness is actually a secret ingredient that helps relationships of different kinds – romantic and platonic – to stand the test of time.

When John Gottman, a scientist famed for his work on relationships, which gave rise to modern-day marriage counselling, observed couples interacting with each another in scientific versions of the "Big Brother House", he found that couples tended to respond to each other in one of two ways.[18]

If one person made a "bid" for connection, the kind of thing we do when we ask for our partner's attention, the other will either "turn toward" or "turn away". Turning toward is when we actively show interest and engage with our partner. Turning away is when we don't, either when we show a lack of interest or even hostility.

When Gottman followed up on the couples years later, he found that those who tended to "turn toward" most of the time were still together. Couples who turned away were not.

Overall, Gottman's research suggests that the magic ratio is 5:1. If we turn toward five times for every time we turn away, a relationship is more likely to last.

EXERCISE:

I Am Grateful to You Because...

1 Make a list of three to five people (or animals) in your life, from the present or the past. These could be parents, grandparents, siblings, friends, colleagues, former teachers or professors, coaches — anyone.

2 Now, write down several reasons why you are grateful to each for their presence in your life. Think about:

💜 How they have impacted your life — how has your life benefited from their presence?

💜 When they have been kind to you, helped you, supported you, believed in you

💜 When you felt happy in their presence

💜 How you have gained from their presence or influence

Consider as many reasons as you can for why you appreciate each person (or animal).

As an alternative version of the exercise, you might even write your reasons as a letter (which you may or may not post).

3. Create a Habit of Kindness

To create a habit of kindness,
we need only make kindness
an intentional, regular practice.

Kindfulness

"Kindfulness" is a blend of being kind and being mindful. It's a bit like mindfulness meditation, except that we don't sit still and passively observe our breathing or thinking, and we become mindful of being kind.

In other words, it means:

💜 Being on the alert for opportunities to be kind

💜 Being kind on purpose – *intentionally* kind

💜 Being kind because it's the right thing to do

💜 Being kind in our thoughts about people

Kindfulness invites us to focus on looking for opportunities to help others. It could be saying or doing something kind at home or work because you realize someone could do with a helping hand, or you spot an opportunity to help someone while you go about your day…and you act on the opportunity.

Kindfulness also calls on us to be kind on purpose, to make a decision to be kind, to be helpful, to try to make our world a little better, or easier, for others by our actions.

Kindfulness asks us to be kind because being kind is the right thing to do. Sometimes, kindness can be fuelled by a sense of expectation or even guilt, and sometimes we help others because we feel it is expected of us. However, kindfulness brings our attention to the fact that what we do is helping another person, regardless of whether it is expected of us or not, and so our kindnesses are done for that reason, because kindness feels like the right thing to do, regardless.

Kindfulness also invites us to be kind in our minds. It invites us to think kindly of people, to try to see the best in them, to look beyond petty annoyances and see the real person underneath, the one who is, like all of us, most likely facing their own challenges.

Exercising the Kindness Muscle

Mindfulness meditation physically impacts the brain. Among other regions, it impacts the prefrontal cortex, above the eyes, causing it to grow like a muscle. This is an area associated with attention. As we learn through mindfulness to place our attention on our breath, for instance, it's as if we take the attention region of the brain to the gym and it grows through neuroplasticity (see page 20).

Any practice performed regularly changes the brain through neuroplasticity. The more we practise, the more the brain changes, the bigger the "muscle" becomes, and the easier it becomes to perform the practice. This applies not only to mindfulness, but to visualization, juggling, running or even playing a musical instrument. A practice of anything shapes the brain in the corresponding region.

And so we can give our brain a work-out, shaping it in positive ways. A mindful practice of kindness builds our brain's kindness muscles.

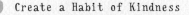

> "A mindful practice of kindness builds our brain's kindness muscles."

As a result, the more we practise kindfulness in its different forms, the better we become at kindfulness, and the easier kindfulness becomes for us.

The Seven-day Kindness Challenge

This exercise helps us to build our kindfulness muscles. The goal is to carry out an act of kindness each day for seven days. Here are a few guidelines to help you to get the most out of the exercise.

1 Try to do something different each day. You can do the same thing on two different days, but it only counts the first time.

2 Try to push yourself out of your comfort zone at least once in the seven days. In other words, do something that stretches you a little.

3 At least one of your kindnesses must be completely anonymous, so no one must know what you did. Or, if it involves a face-to-face kind act, no one you know must find out what you did. There is a reason for pushing ourselves out of our comfort zone. Just as stretching at yoga improves the range and flexibility of our muscles, making subsequent stretches easier, so it is the same with kindness. Pushing ourselves out of our comfort zone stretches us a little and makes it easier in future to do the same kinds of things. Ultimately, it widens the range of kindnesses we are able (and willing) to do.

If you make it through seven days, see if you can follow the exercise for three weeks. This time, it's OK to count the same kindness twice, but only if they are spaced apart by at least a week.

Also, if you've gone seven days, try to push yourself out of your comfort zone just once more in the next two weeks and do one more anonymous act of kindness too.

The 365-day Kindness Challenge

If you're up for it, why not try to go a full year? You'll need a diary for this one, because it's a great exercise to record the kind things you do, whether they are simply a few kind words or a full act of kindness.

The guidelines are a little more relaxed than they are for seven days: there's no need to push yourself out of your comfort zone or do acts anonymously. These will happen by themselves through the year. Just try to vary your kind acts as much as you can. This is easier than you might think because, as your "kindness muscle" grows, you will be alert to more opportunities to be kind and you will find it easier to act on them.

4. Be Kind to Yourself

It is very important that we remember to be kind to ourselves. Being kind to ourselves is part of valuing ourselves and also gives us more energy to be able to be kind to others.

Self-care

Being kind to others doesn't mean we must always put others before ourselves. Self-care is not a matter of "care for yourself instead of others", nor "care for yourself once you've finished caring for others" nor "at the same time as you care for others". It's not even "care for yourself before caring for others". It's just self-care. We complicate things too much in our own minds. It's simply about respecting your own needs and desires.

Self-care might sometimes mean saying "no", or at least "not yet" or "maybe later". We're not being unkind here, but simply recognizing that we sometimes need to refuel, to re-energize ourselves, so that we are better able to live our lives and take care of our responsibilities. Self-care allows us to recharge so we have more energy to be kind.

Saying "no" from time to time can help increase mental and emotional energy so that we are able to say "yes" on many other occasions.

If we don't look after our own needs and therefore our own energy levels, we become drained or burned out through over-giving, just like a battery drains if overused. Ultimately, while we might feel like we're helping in the short-term, in the long-term we wear ourselves out.

Being kind to ourselves can also mean leaving an abusive or controlling relationship, or quitting a job because of stress, bullying or simply because it doesn't inspire us and we know we deserve to do work that lights us up. It can mean removing ourselves from a set of circumstances that drains us.

Being kind to ourselves can also mean treating ourselves because we deserve it. We needn't justify it. Whether it's through the purchase of something we want or giving ourselves a special day, an experience or even a holiday, being kind to ourselves reminds us that we're "worth it".

What Can I Do for Myself? Because I'm Worth It!

1 Make a list of self-care things you could do. List as many as you wish, even those you think might not be possible (yet). If you're struggling for ideas, here are a few that might get you thinking:

💜 Schedule some time for yourself

💜 Say "no"

💜 Go for a walk

💜 Take a hot bath

💜 Go on a spa day

💜 Treat yourself to something you've wanted for a while

💜 Visit a place you don't often have a chance to go to, or have never been to before

💜 Spend time with friends

💜 Go out for the evening

💜 Attend a yoga or meditation class

♥ Prepare a favourite meal for yourself

♥ Get your hair cut

♥ Wear your favourite outfit just because you feel like it

♥ Turn your phone off for a few hours

♥ Sit in the park and read a book

2 Narrow your list down now. Select three things that you intend to do for yourself in the next month. Include one that you could do within the next week. Select an extra one that you intend to do within the next year.

Self-compassion Boosts Self-esteem

Part of being kind to ourselves is self-compassion, which is the feeling of being sympathetic and understanding toward ourselves, of being patient with ourselves, even of being moved by our own suffering.

- Self-compassion understands that we can't be perfect, that we can't win or succeed all the time

- With self-compassion, we understand that having a bad day isn't a failure but a normal part of being human

- Self-compassion is like a soft place to land when things get tough

- Self-compassion says, "I am good enough, just as I am."

- Self-compassion silences the self-critical voice that many of us have learned to listen to and replaces it with a softer, wiser voice, a voice whose main message is, "You're doing great. Everything will be fine."

- Self-compassion boosts our self-esteem

Self-compassion Improves Mental Health

Like kindness to others, self-compassion can be an antidote to depression, especially if depression is fuelled by thoughts of failure, not being good enough or even self-loathing.

Self-compassion understands that it's perfectly fine to be exactly as you are, with your history as it is, with the qualifications and experience you have, with the way you look, your weight, your shape and any other attribute you tend to criticize.

Studies on self-compassion find that even the inner voices of the best self-critics can be silenced and replaced by understanding, acceptance and patience. It can even help us find a little more happiness. As self-criticism is replaced with self-compassion, emotional blocks to happiness are often dissolved and we discover a fountain of well-being that's always been there, ready to face the sunshine.

"Self-compassion can be an antidote to depression."

Self-compassion as an Anti-inflammatory

The vagus nerve is the longest cranial nerve in the body, working its way through the face, throat, heart, lungs and all of our organs.

It plays a key role in the rest and digest portion of the nervous system. You can feel its action when you take your pulse. Pulse rate quickens a little on the in breath, only to slow down on the out breath. The slowing down is the work of the vagus nerve.

The vagus nerve also slows inflammation in what is known as the inflammatory reflex. Inflammation is the redness and swelling that occur when a wound is healing. It is a vital part of the immune response and helps attract blood and nutrients to a wound site to aid the healing process. But most inflammation occurs on the inside of the body: throughout the cardiovascular system, the immune system and the joints. This internal inflammation is often a consequence of stress, poor lifestyle choices and even environmental factors.

Inflammation is known to play a role in cardiovascular disease, cancer, arthritis and even Alzheimer's.

Self-compassion as well as compassion for others are linked with the vagus nerve. The connection is known as polyvagal theory, first conceived by Stephen Porges, Director of the Brain–Body Center at the University of Illinois. Numerous studies have shown that vagal tone, akin to muscle tone and an indicator of vagus nerve activity, increases as we build compassion for ourselves and compassion for others.[19] The increase in vagal tone is also related to a subsequent decrease in inflammation.

In a study led by scientists at Emory University in Atlanta, for example, volunteers practised a compassion-based meditation for six weeks, which included focus on self-compassion as well as compassion for others.[20] The scientists measured plasma inflammation levels before and after the six weeks of practice and found that the compassion meditation practice significantly reduced inflammation levels.

Inflamm-aging

As well as playing a role in many diseases, inflammation also plays a big role in the disease of aging. So much so that Claudio Franceschi, an inflammation expert and professor at the University of Bologna, has begun to refer to it as "inflammaging". The term has caught on among scientists, some of whom hyphenate it to "inflamm-aging".

However, if self-compassion and compassion for others can reduce inflammation, then they must also slow aging on the inside of the body. Perhaps the elusive elixir of life has never truly been discovered because we have never thought to seek it inside ourselves, in our capacity to care.

Self-compassion and compassion for others *are* the elixir of life.

Cultivating Self-compassion

The object of this exercise is to learn to listen to our inner Buddha – our wisest, most compassionate self – and replace a self-critical voice with a self-compassionate voice. Self-criticism isn't natural to us. It's a learned habit, and we've merely learned to listen to that voice. Through following this exercise, the dominant feelings of self-criticism or hurt will gradually be replaced by self-compassion.

1 Take some paper and three pens of different colours. Decide on a pen for each of three inner voices. Use one pen for the voice of the inner critic, another for the voice of your hurt self when you feel criticized. The third pen is for the voice of your inner Buddha.

2 Start a three-way dialogue between the three voices. Begin with the voice of the self-critic. Write down exactly what it says, the words you use to describe yourself when you are being self-critical or mean to yourself. Write as much as you wish.

3 Then change to the pen for your hurt self and write a response to the inner critic. Write down how you feel about those words and what you want to say back.

4 When you're ready, introduce your inner Buddha, representing your deepest, wisest, most understanding and compassionate self. Write a response to the words of both the inner critic and your hurt self.

5 You can continue a three-way dialogue for as long as you feel is necessary, covering several pages if you need to. Write about how you truly feel and allow your inner Buddha's wisdom to infuse the pages. Each time you feel your inner Buddha is about to speak, take time to imagine what this fountain of wisdom and compassion would say. At the conclusion of the exercise, let the inner Buddha have the last word.

The Loving-kindness Meditation (see page 22) is also a very good exercise for developing self-compassion.

5. Kindness is Contagious

Anything that spreads is contagious. We usually think of the word contagious in the context of a cold or a disease of some sort. Actually, kindness is one of the *most* contagious things.

The Ripple Effect of Kindness

Just as a pebble dropped in a pond creates waves that lift lily pads all around the pond, so acts of kindness do the same thing, although kindness lifts spirits instead of lily pads. Buoyed by kindness shown to us, we often show kindness to others as a result, thus facilitating the spread of the wave.

This "pay it forward" effect seems to be caused by "elevation", defined by Jonathan Haidt, Professor of Ethical Leadership at New York University, as a sense of warmth, gratitude, connection, openness or expansion that we feel when someone is kind to us. In research studies, Haidt has shown that when people feel elevated as a consequence of receiving or witnessing kindness, they are motivated to be kind themselves.

Three Degrees of Separation

Just as a wave spreads out in all directions, a person receiving kindness is very often kind to more than one person. This spreading-out effect has been tracked to three degrees of separation by James Fowler, a geneticist and social scientist at the University of California, San Diego, and Nicholas Christakis, a professor of social and natural science at Yale. [21]

In business game simulations, Fowler and Christakis have shown that an act of kindness tends to spread out to at least "three degrees of separation", or three social steps.

You may be familiar with the six-degree rule, meaning that every person in the world is connected to any other person by six social steps or less. In kindness terms, this means:

One degree – A person you show kindness to is considered one degree of separation away from you. When you are kind to them, they are more likely to be kind (or kinder) to someone else.

Two degrees – This "someone else" is two degrees (or two "social steps") away from you. You may have never met this person, yet they are benefiting from something kind that you said or did. This person is then likely to be kind (or kinder) to someone else.

Three degrees – This "someone else" is three degrees, or social steps, away from you. In all likelihood you have never met, nor will ever meet, this person, yet they are benefiting from your act of kindness. This person is then likely to be kind (or kinder) to someone else (who is technically four degrees away from you, but your kind act is altering the behaviour of the person three degrees away from you).

Kindness is Contagious 85

So, for example, you might be kind to someone (1),

…who later that day shows extra kindness to a work colleague (2),

…who then acts on a later opportunity to help a woman carry her pram up a flight of stairs (3),

…who then gives some money to a homeless person.

While it seems completely unrelated on the surface, the woman received a helping hand with her pram and the homeless person received some money because of your first act of kindness.

In practice, however, the people at two and three degrees of separation from you will be kind or kinder to more than one person over the course of a day. This is what Fowler and Christakis found.

Let's say the average number of people that each person is kind (or kinder) to is four. It means that your single act of kindness will actually impact $4\times4\times4 = 64$ people. If the number were five, it would mean that your single act of kindness will impact $5\times5\times5 = 125$ people. The real number will vary from place to place, but you can rest assured that almost every act of kindness spreads out in this way.

If you ever doubted your impact on society or even the world, if you ever felt that you didn't matter or made a contribution to the world, just reflect on these very real numbers. If you want to make a difference, be kind!

That's all it takes.
Let elevation do the rest.

"A person receiving kindness is very often kind to more than one person."

EXERCISE:

Seek Out Opportunities to Be Kind

Make an effort to simply be on the lookout for opportunities to be kind to people. Just making the clear and simple decision to do so will help you spot things you might have missed before.

As you go about your day, from the time you get out of bed, on your way to work, throughout the day at work, on the way home and at home in the evening, be nice, be kind, smile at others, pay people genuine compliments.

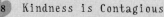

Conclusion:
Kindness Works

With enough compassion
and kindness in our hearts,
we can change the world.

Inspired by the ripple effect of kindness, I have believed for many years that with enough compassion and kindness in our hearts, we can change the world.

I believe we all can make a difference in the world. It's our world; we just need to see it that way and take some personal responsibility for it. For the planet, it might be in the way we choose to lead our lives, in the products we consume, in the amount of plastic we use, or any of a multitude of other practical ways. In this book, I have focused on kindness to others (and self) as a vehicle for positive change. But it's not all about making the world a better place.

"I believe we all can make a difference in the world."

In reality, an act of kindness is about making something a little better for the person (or animal) standing right in front of you. We do kindness mostly without considering a bigger picture, simply because kindness is the right thing to do.

The ripple effect is a side effect. It is one of the side effects of kindness. I have written about other side effects of kindness throughout this book. One of the reasons I share science is that I have learned that science brings a unique dimension to kindness and it gets people talking about it more. And when people talk about it more, it comes more into vogue and so more people are inspired to be kind.

My passion is to be an advocate of kindness, to do my bit to expand the discussion of kindness and its importance in the public consciousness.

On a practical level, I am not the kindest person. I am just an ordinary person, like you, with my own faults, trying to do my little bit from my own corner of the universe. I'm also trying to grasp how we are all in this together – life lived on our shared planet.

For we are all in this together, this thing called life. Why not do what we can to make the experience a little happier for people? Not by neglecting ourselves, of course, but in addition to catering for our own needs and desires.

Consider this: everyone creates this world. If we help make things better for others, we come to live in the societies that they help create. Or, to play with a well-known phrase, if you pee in the pool, you have to swim in the pool. But acts of kindness here and there are like cleaning the pool and giving others the energy to help clean it too. In time, we all swim in a clean pool.

No man is an island, they say. No one is separate from the pool.

I am hopeful that you have enjoyed reading this book, that it might get you thinking, that it might result in you helping to make a moment or two of someone's life a little bit easier or more enjoyable.

Let us do what we can for each other.

Let us be kind.

References

Chapter 1

1 E B Raposa et al., "Prosocial behaviour mitigates the negative effects of stress in everyday life", *Clinical Psychological Science*, 2015, 4(4), 691–698

2 A Lutz et al, "Regulation of the neural circuitry of emotion by compassion meditation: Effects of meditative experience", *PLoS ONE*, 2008, 3(3), e1897; M Engström and B Söderfeldt, "Brain activation during compassion meditation", *The Journal of Alternative and Complementary Medicine*, 2010, 16(5), 597–599

3 S Israel et al., "The oxytocin receptor (OXTR) contributes to prosocial fund allocations in the Dictator Game and the social value orientations task", *PLoS ONE*, 2009, 4 (5), e5535

4 www.bucharestearlyintervention project.org

Chapter 2

5 S Lyubomirsky et al, "Pursuing sustained happiness through random acts of kindness and counting one's blessings: Tests of two six-week interventions", Department of Psychology, University of California, Riverside, unpublished data, 2004

6 T Taubes, "Healthy avenues of the mind: psychological theory building and the influence of religion during the era of moral treatment", *American Journal of Psychiatry*, 1998, 155, 1,001–8

7 M A Musick and J Wilson, "Volunteering and depression: the role of psychological and social resources in different age groups", *Social Science and Medicine*, 2003, 56(2), 259–69

8 P Petrovic, R Kalisch, T Singer and R Dolan, "Oxytocin attenuates affective evaluations of conditioned faces and amygdala activity", *Journal of Neuroscience*, 2008, 28 (26), 2008, 6607–15

9 For the cardioprotective effect of oxytocin, see: M Jankowski, T L Broderick and J Gutkowska, "Oxytocin and cardioprotection in diabetes and obesity", *BMC Endocrine Disorders*, 2016, 16, 34; and M Jankowski, A Gonzalez-Reyes, N Noiseux and J Gutkowska, "Oxytocin in the heart regeneration", *Recent Patents on Cardiovascular Drug Discovery*, 2012, 7, 81–7

10 T W Smith et al., "Marital conflict behaviour and coronary artery calcification", Paper presented at the American Psychosomatic Society's 64th Annual Meeting, Denver, CO, 3 March 2006

11 A Szeto et al., "Oxytocin attenuates NADP-dependent superoxide activity and IL-6 secretion in macrophages and vascular cells", *American Journal of Endocrinology and Metabolism*, 2008, 295, E1495–1501

12 K C Light et al., "More frequent partner hugs and higher oxytocin levels are linked to lower blood pressure and heart rate in premenopausal women", *Biological Psychology*, 2005, 69, 5–21; K M Grewen et al., "Effects of partner support on resting oxytocin, cortisol, norepinephrine, and blood pressure before and after warm partner contact", *Psychosomatic Medicine*, 67, 2005, 531–8

13 G N Levine et al., "Pet ownership and cardiovascular risk: a scientific statement from the American Heart Association", *Circulation*, 2013, 127(123), 2353-2363

14 E Friedmann and S A Thomas, "Pet ownership, social support, and one-year survival after acute myocardial infarction in the Cardiac Arrhythmia Suppression Trial (CAST)", *American Journal of Cardiology*, 1995, 76, 1,213–17

15 M Nagasawa et al., "Oxytocin-gaze positive loop and the coevolution of human dog bonds", *Science*, 348(6232), 333–336. The levels rose by over 300% during a 30-minute period.

16 D C McClelland and C Kirshnit, "The effect of motivational arousal through films on salivary immunoglobulin A", *Psychology and Health*, 1988, 2(1), 31–52

17 For the effect of oxytocin on skin cells, see V Deing et al., "Oxytocin modulates proliferation and stress responses of human skin cells: implications for atopic dermatitis", *Experimental Dermatology*, 2013, 22(6), 399–405

18 J M Gottman, *What Predicts Divorce? The Relationship between Marital Processes and Marital Outcomes*, Psychology Press, 1993

Chapter 4

19 B E Kok et al., "How positive emotions build physical health: perceived positive social connections account for the upward spiral between positive emotions and vagal tone", *Psychological Science*, 2013, 24(7), 1,123–32

20 T W W Pace et al., "Effect of compassion meditation on neuroendocrine, innate immune and behavioural responses to psychosocial stress", *Psychoneuroendocrinology*, 2009, 34, 87–98

Chapter 5

21 J H Fowler and N A Christakis, "Cooperative behaviour cascades in human social networks", *Proceedings of the National Academy of Sciences*, 2010, 107(12), 5,334–8

Acknowledgments

Writing can be a solitary job, but at the same time a writer is richly connected to all the people who play a role in her or his life. I would not be able to write books at all were it not for the love and support of a great many people.

My partner, Elizabeth Caproni, shows me kindness every day. That I can even say I am an author is mostly because of the help and support I have received from her over the years.

My mum and dad have been great teachers to me, not just in what they say, but in what they do. I have learned kindness by being on the receiving end of it on more occasions than I could possibly count. Their love and kindness toward me have shaped the very essence of this book.

To all the scientists who did the research presented in this book: the world is a better place because of the work you do.

I'd also like to thank Leanne Bryan at Octopus for first proposing the idea of this book, and all the staff at Octopus who have helped throughout the process.

Caffe Nero in Stirling, Scotland, also deserve a special mention because I wrote the majority of this book there. I appreciate the atmosphere the staff create and the friendliness they have always shown toward me.